Jesus Walked in Our Shoes

RICKY CLEMONS

PUBLISHED BY FIEDLI PUBLISHING, INC.

Copyright ©2020, Ricky Clemons

ALL RIGHTS RESERVED.

No part of this publication may be reproduced, stored in a retrieval system, or transmitted in any form or by any means—electronic, mechanical, photo-copy, recording, or any other—except for brief quotation in reviews, without the prior permission of the author or publisher.

ISBN: 978-1-60414-972-2

Published by

Fideli Publishing, Inc.
119 W. Morgan St.
Martinsville, IN 46151

www.FideliPublishing.com

Contents

Jesus Walked in Our Shoes 1
The Living Church 3
To be a Believer in Jesus Christ. 5
There is a God 7
Love 9
We Can Surely Love One Another 11
Birds Will Flock Together 13
Only God Knows the Heart 15
Blessings 17
Spiritual Maturity 19
We Can Change Like the Seasons 21
I Need You So Much, O Lord 23
Life Will Survive 25
The Lord is Always on Time 27
Money 29
The Darkness of Sin 31
Off the Face of the Earth 33
Insecure 35
Fear 37
Do We Crucify Jesus Today? 39
Carnal-minded People 41
Any One of Us 43

I Took a Lot of Chances	44
Children	45
Your Marvelous Gospel	46
If Jesus is Not in It	47
Your Holy Word	48
Dreams and Reality	49
Who Can Answer Jesus' Questions?	50
Life Doesn't	51
Yesterday, Today, and Tomorrow	52
Who Am I to Question You, My Lord	53
The Sky Hovers Over	54
A Dark World	55
Jesus is Bigger Than the Storm	56
Everlasting	57
You Were with Me	58
I am a Christian Black Man	59
Keeping God's Commandments	63
It's No Mistake	65
Rich with Spiritual Things	67
Deep Within Ourselves	69
Actions	71
Common Sense	73
Jesus Didn't Let the Devil Kill Me	76
The Sleeping Saints	78

My Lord and Savior Jesus Christ.. 79
You are So Good to Me... 80
It Means Nothing Much at All If Jesus is Not in It...................... 81
Our Faith is Being Tested 82

Jesus Walked in Our Shoes

Jesus walked in our shoes when he lived on earth.

He was tempted by the devil in many ways that we will never be tempted.

Jesus knows what it feels like to be rejected.

Jesus knows what it feels like to be falsely accused.

Jesus knows what it feels like to be depressed.

Jesus knows what it feels like to be put down.

Jesus knows what it feels like to be hungry.

Jesus knows what it feels like to be to be insulted.

Jesus shed some tears.

Jesus knows what it feels like to be denied.

Jesus knows what it feels like to be called a liar.

Jesus knows what it feels like to be hurt.

Jesus knows what it feels like to be sad.

Jesus knows what it feels like to be despised.

Jesus knows what it feels like to suffer.

Jesus knows what it feels like to be knocked down.

Jesus knows what it feels like to be discouraged.

Jesus knows what it feels like to be disappointed.

Jesus Christ, our Lord and Savior, walked in our shoes that we will never deserve.

All the bad things that we go through in life are nothing compared to what Jesus went through for us.

He didn't have to do it, but He did it to save us from our sins.

The devil came at Jesus with all of his temptations, but they failed to cause Jesus to sin against his heavenly Father who Jesus got His strength from.

All that we say and do should honor and glorify Jesus Christ, our Lord.

Jesus knows what it feels like to feel alone.

Jesus knows what it feels like to feel abandoned.

Jesus knows what it feels like to be belittled.

Jesus knows what it feels like to be homeless.

Jesus knows what it feels like to be poor.

Jesus knows what it feels like to be tired.

Jesus knows what it feels like to not be loved.

Jesus knows what it feels like to grieve.

Jesus walked in our shoes, and that wasn't easy for Him to do because our shoes are flawed in sin when Jesus has no sin.

The Living Church

The Living Church is you and me, who are alive to worship and pray to our Lord and Savior Jesus Christ.

We should live our lives loving and obeying Jesus Christ.

We are the Living Church body of Jesus Christ.

We can talk about the Lord and walk here and there to spread the gospel of Jesus Christ.

The material church building has windows that can crack and break into pieces.

The church building has walls that can dry rot and fall apart.

The church building has floors that can get lumpy and uneven.

The church building has a rooftop that can leak and fall in.

The church building has doors that can be knocked down and can swell up.

The church building has church pews that can fade.

The church building can't worship the Lord.

The church building can't pray to the Lord.

The church building can't love and obey the Lord.

The church building can't walk house to house to spread the gospel of Jesus Christ.

The church building has no life to live unto Jesus Christ.

The Living Church is you and me who have lives to live unto our Lord and Savior Jesus Christ.

The church building is only a symbol of you and me who are the real, true church.

We are the Living Church of Jesus Christ our Lord.

We are the living bride to have a relationship with Jesus Christ.

We are the real, true church bride to be married to Jesus Christ.

The church building can't have a relationship with Jesus Christ.

The church building can't be married to Jesus Christ.

The church building is only a material thing that can't choose right from wrong.

We are the real, true Living Church.

We can choose to live right unto the Lord with the help of the Holy Spirit.

The Holy Spirit lives in you and me, not in the church building that criminals can walk into and kill you and me.

The government and state can shut the church building down, but they can't shut our hearts down and keep us from worshipping and obeying the Lord.

To be a Believer in Jesus Christ.

To be a believer in Jesus Christ we must believe that He is the Son of God.

We must believe that He is the light of the world.

We must believe that He is the living word of God.

We must believe that He is the creator of all things.

We must believe that He is the prince of peace.

We must believe that He is the wonderful counselor.

We must believe that He is the beginning and the end.

We must believe that He is I am that I am.

We must believe that He is the rock of all ages.

We must believe that He is the ancient of days.

We must believe that He is our refuge.

We must believe that He is our sword and shield.

We must believe that He cannot fail us.

We must believe that He will forgive us of our sins.

If we confess and repent, we must believe that He will cleanse us of our sins.

If we confess and repent, we must believe that He will save us from our sins.

We must believe that He will save us from our sins.

We must believe that He is the way, truth and life.

We must believe that He is the resurrection.

To be a believer of Jesus Christ we must believe that He is coming back again.

To be a believer of Jesus Christ we must believe that He will give us the victory to win.

we must believe that He will give us strength.

We must believe that He will help us.

We must believe that He will bless us.

We must believe that He will never leave us or forsake us.

We must believe that He is the bright and morning star.

We must believe that He is the lily in the valley.

We must believe that He will give us eternal life.

We must believe that He keeps His promises.

We must believe that He is our judge.

We must believe that He is our advocate.

We must believe that He is our protector.

We must believe that He is our defender.

We must believe that He is our Lord and Savior.

We must believe that He is our God.

There is a God

It's an extraordinary thing that we are still in the land of the living.

Who are we to say that we are still here because of living right unto the Lord?

We can easily believe that our living right unto the Lord is in our favor.

Many good people have passed away when they were young, middle aged and old.

Could we say that they didn't love the Lord Jesus Christ?

It is like a mystery to me that I am still alive, when many Christian people are gone to the grave.

Many of them were very young and loved the Lord.

Just because we are Christians, it doesn't mean that we deserve to live a long life in the land of the living.

The Lord shows no favoritism to those he wants to keep alive or allow to die, no matter what their age.

It is extraordinary that we are still alive in a world where there are over a thousand ways to die.

Whoever is alive and believes that there is no God is truly fooling themselves into believing that lie.

If lies exist, then surely God exists, because He cannot lie.

There is a God who is keeping you and me alive.

Nothing can be more extraordinary than God.

All the good that we do can't keep us alive.

We know that accidents happen that can kill us.

Accidents can show up out of nowhere at any time of the day or night.

We have no control over accidents.

God is more real than any accident, and He protects you and me from the accidents that can take our lives.

We are so blessed that there is a God who causes us to still exist.

Many people believe they are self-made and are keeping themselves alive.

A fool in his heart will believe that there is no God, until death knocks him down off his high horse.

God gives us life, and even a fool likes to live and won't brag about wanting to die.

We Christians believe that there is a God, whether we live a long or a short life.

There is a God who decides how long He wants us to live.

God also decides how long He wants a fool to live, even though the fool believes that there is no God.

Love

Love will make us feel so good.

Love will never give us ill feelings.

Love gives us strength to keep going.

Love will never be rude to us.

Love heals a broken heart.

Love will never abandon us.

Love won't cause us to do anything wrong.

Love will never spitefully use us.

Love doesn't hold grudges.

Love will never ignore us.

Love doesn't give up on us.

Love brings us together on one accord.

Love gives us another chance.

Love makes no conflicts.

Love will never let us down.

Love won't wear us out.

Love will never be cruel to us.

Love is patient with us.

Love won't try to control us.

Love is always normal in this sin-sick world.

Love will never criticize us.

Love gives us all equal opportunities.

Love will treat us all right.

Love will never verbally abuse us.

Love will never emotionally abuse us.

Love will never physically abuse us.

Love will stand by us.

Love will lift us up when we are feeling down.

Love is always real with us.

Love will never deceive us.

Love tells us the truth in love.

Love opens our eyes to see the light.

Love will never pretend with us.

Love is for us and not against us.

Love is very sure to make our lives better.

Love is God.

Love is Jesus Christ.

Love is the Holy Spirit.

We Can Surely Love One Another

I have two little dogs that I live with; one is a boy dog and the other is a girl.

The boy is pretty laid back and doesn't get into things.

The girl dog is a little busybody.

She likes to get into everything.

Sometimes, I will leave the house and leave them out of their cage.

One day, I left the house to go to the store.

I left them out of their cage, and when I got back home there were paper napkins laying all over the floor.

I knew right away who did it.

I still showed her some love, even though I didn't like what she did.

Another week passed by, and I went out to the store again.

I left the two dogs out of their cage, and when I got back home, the leather that was on my ink pen had been chewed up.

Again, I knew right away who did it.

I still showed my girl dog some love, even though I didn't like what she had done.

If I can show a dog some love, even when it misbehaves, I can surely show some love to a human being who is created in the image of God.

The Lord commands you and me to love one another and forgive one another.

If I can forgive my dog, then I can surely forgive a human being who may say something or do something I don't like.

Many people love their animals much more than they love human beings who can learn from their mistakes.

A dog can't learn from their mistakes.

A dog will keep on doing the wrong thing over and over again.

A dog doesn't have a mind to know right from wrong.

Especially we brothers and sisters in the church can love one another.

We want to be like Jesus Christ, who loves everybody.

Birds Will Flock Together

Birds will flock together in any kind of weather.

We brothers and sisters in Jesus Christ can come together in worshipping the Lord on His holy sabbath day of rest.

We can come together to listen to the sermons that the pastor and elders preach about Jesus Christ.

We brothers and sisters in Jesus Christ can come together in prayer unto the Lord.

The more that people are praying, the more power we will receive from the Lord.

Birds will flock together no matter where they fly to.

They all will land on the ground together and find food to eat.

We brothers and sisters in Jesus Christ can come together in bible study, even though we are all different and come from different walks of life.

We can all come together in agreement with God's holy word, even though we have different experiences in life.

We brothers and sisters in Jesus Christ can come together in sharing our spiritual gifts with one another.

We all can be blessed by one another's spiritual gift uplift one another in our Lord and Savior Jesus Christ.

We brothers and sisters in Jesus Christ can come together and go out in the streets to reach lost people with the good news about Jesus Christ, who brought his disciples together to go out and heal the sick, cast out demons and do many other things in Jesus' holy and precious name.

Birds will flock together because Jesus created them to be that way.

Jesus created us to come together in our new spiritual birth of being born again and being spiritually minded.

The birds will flock together to be a good example for us to be one body in Jesus Christ.

The birds need each other to help fight off their predators who attack them.

We need each other to help protect one another's souls and to hold on to Jesus Christ and do His holy will.

We brothers and sisters in Jesus Christ can come together through the Holy Spirit, even though we are different like the parts of our bodies that work together to allow the whole body to function normally.

Only God Knows the Heart

We can live with someone for years and really not know that person.

We can live next door to someone and really not know that person.

We can work right next to someone on the job and really not know that person.

We can go to church and really not know anyone in the church.

We may know someone's name, but we don't know what's in that person's heart.

We don't know what someone is thinking.

We don't know how someone feels, unless that person tells us.

We don't know what is on someone's mind, unless that person tells us.

We can't know what is in someone's heart.

We can think that we know and we may be so wrong.

Thoughts are unseen and every thought is not revealed in an action.

Every parent may not really know their child.

Many people will conceal who they really are.

Many people will conceal their true selves for years and years.

We don't really know ourselves.

We don't know what we will think before we think it.

We don't always know what we will say before we say it.

We don't always know what we will do before we do it.

Only God knows us completely day after day.

God knows what's in our hearts every day.

We will fall short of truly knowing ourselves.

We can surprise other people and even surprise ourselves.

The heart can be unpredictable.

The heart can be so unknown to you and me.

Many men will pretend to love their wives, when they don't love them at all.

Many women will pretend to love their husbands, when they don't love them.

They can go through the motions of loving them, but their love is not true.

Many people will have a relationship with someone and not really know that person.

Many people will get married and not really know their spouse.

When they do this, they may find out later down the road that they made a big mistake.

Only God knows our hearts, because we can never fool God.

Blessings

The Lord can bless us in some ways that we don't ask Him to bless us.

We can't see all the blessings that the Lord gives to us.

The Lord's blessings are always good for us to receive.

We don't deserve any of His blessings because we're born in sin.

The Lord will sometimes bless us when we don't expect it.

We don't always know how blessed we are.

Some people are more blessed than others, and we don't always know why.

Many wicked people are blessed with many material things.

The Lord loves them too, but hates their sins.

Many Christian people are poor and don't have much.

Many Christian people don't have many material things, but they are so blessed with spiritual things.

Many people will worship their blessings and will not worship the Lord who gives them their blessings.

Blessings are always a good thing.

There is nothing bad about being blessed.

There are people who will envy you and me if they see that we are blessed by the Lord.

When have blessings ever made anyone angry?

When have blessings ever made anyone sad?

When have blessings ever made anyone unhappy?

Many people will get selfish when they are blessed.

Many people will get proud when they are blessed

Many people will change for the worse when they are blessed.

Many people will believe that they are better than others when they are blessed.

There is no evil in blessings.

Many people will do evil things when they are blessed, and use that blessing for worldly gain.

Many people will put their blessings above the Lord who gave them the blessings.

The devil can't bless anyone, but he will try to use our blessings to cause us to believe that we are self-made.

Spiritual Maturity

We all need more spiritual maturity in the Lord.

The Lord gives us spiritual gifts, but that doesn't mean we don't need to improve on those spiritual gifts.

There are Christians who have a lot of bible knowledge, but that doesn't mean they have experienced a spiritual walk through the scriptures.

The Lord has brought us all a long way to become spiritual adults in His holy word, but that doesn't mean we don't need some spiritual maturity.

We must go through some trials in life to test our faith in Jesus Christ.

As some people may say, talk is cheap.

We don't want our talk to be cheap about our Lord and Savior Jesus Christ who has walked in all of our shoes so we can spiritually walk beyond our talk about Him.

The truth can set us free.

There is always more truth that we need to know about the Lord.

When we believe that we understand the bible scriptures to the fullest, the Lord can allow us to go through an experience to see what a scripture truly means.

We all need more spiritual maturity in the Lord.

A lifetime of maturing has to wait on us to get where the Lord needs us to be.

We do this through confessing our sins and repenting unto Him as much as we have breath in our bodies to do so.

We all need more spiritual maturity in the Lord.

We can't spiritually mature at all without the Holy Spirit that gives us spiritual gifts.

We can study the bible over and over again, but without the Holy Spirit, our eyes won't see the spiritual things that the Lord wants to reveal to us.

We Can Change Like the Seasons

We can change like the seasons.

Life can surely take us through some changes.

We change our minds sometimes.

Some people change their minds a lot.

We have no control over change.

Our feelings can change over the years.

Our bodies can change over the years.

We will go through some changes in our lives as we get older.

We will always change in some ways.

Changes can sometimes be a good thing for our well-being.

We know that the seasons will change, and that is a good thing.

If it was the spring season all year 'round, so many people would have allergies.

If it was the summer season all year 'round, so many people would have sunburns.

If it was the fall season all year 'round, so many people would have fever blisters.

We could have a good experience that could change our lives.

We could have a bad experience that could change our lives.

We could say something and then change what we say.

We can have a change of heart about something.

Our behavior can change when we go through some hardships in life.

Changes can make us wise.

Changes can make many people foolish.

Anyone's life can change for the better if they believe in Jesus Christ.

Anyone's life will change for the better for loving and obeying Jesus.

The government and states can change laws.

God will never change His holy law.

God will never change His holy word.

People can change on you and me, but God doesn't change.

The things in this world will change like the seasons, but God will never change.

I Need You So Much, O Lord

I need you so much today, O Lord, that will take a gamble on my life like playing a high-stake game of cards.

I need you so much today, O Lord, on this day that can cheat me out of my life.

I need you so much today, O Lord, on this day that can throw a fast curve ball at me.

I need you so much today, O Lord, on this day that can mess me around.

I need you so much today, O Lord, on this day that can shoot me down.

I need you so much today, O Lord, on this day that can blow a fuse on me.

I need you so much today, O Lord, on this day that can come to me empty handed.

I need you so much today, O Lord, on this day that can kick me around.

I need you so much today, O Lord, on this day that can get drunk on me.

I need you so much today, O Lord, on this day that can wear me out.

I need you so much today, O Lord, on this day that can give me grief.

I need you so much today, O Lord, on this day that can break my heart.

I need you so much today, O Lord, on this day that can break its promise to me.

I need you so much today, O Lord, on this day that can disappoint me.

I need you so much today, O Lord, on this day that can hold a grudge against me.

I need you so much today, O Lord, on this day that can chew me up.

I need you so much today, O Lord, on this day that can do me wrong.

I need you so much today, O Lord, on this day that can let me down.

I need you so much today, O Lord, on this day that can be my fate.

I need you so much today, O Lord, on this day that can show me that there is no tomorrow for me to see.

I need you so much today, O Lord, on this day that I want to live my life unto You.

No matter what today may bring me, today can't stop me from using my free will to love and obey You, my Lord and Savior Jesus Christ.

Today can't do more to me, O Lord, than what you allow it to do.

Today can't go over its limit with you in my corner, O Lord.

Life Will Survive

No matter how many people die, life will survive.

Life will go on from day to day, because life was destined to always exist.

From one generation to the next generation, it goes on starting in a mother's womb.

Life will survive regardless of wars.

Life will survive regardless of diseases.

Life will survive regardless of famines.

Life will survive regardless of natural disasters.

Life will survive regardless of death.

Life will survive because Jesus Christ is life eternal.

Jesus is life, and all life comes from Him.

Life will survive regardless of viruses.

Life will survive regardless of murders.

Life will survive regardless of sickness.

Life will survive regardless of droughts.

Life will survive regardless of starvation.

Life will survive regardless of homelessness.

Life will survive regardless of accidents.

Life will survive regardless of mistakes.

Life will survive forever and ever beyond this sinful world.

Sin can't destroy life because of God who lives forever and ever on His holy throne.

Life will always outlast death; Jesus will put an end to death one day.

There would be no history without life existing in the past.

There would be no prophecy without life existing in the future.

There would be no you and me without life existing in the present.

Life will survive regardless of you and me who will one day die if Jesus Christ doesn't come back during our lifetimes.

We will pray and hope that we are saved in Him when He comes back.

We don't want to be among the wicked living who will drop dead at the appearance of Jesus Christ.

Life will survive regardless of earthquakes that will happen when Jesus comes back again.

The Lord is Always on Time

The Lord is always on time to help us.

The Lord is always on time to protect us.

The Lord is always on time to speak to us.

The Lord is always on time to rescue us.

The Lord always spoke to his prophets on time.

The Lord created the heavens on time.

The Lord created the earth on time.

The Lord created the angels on time.

The Lord created the Adam and Eve on time.

The Lord will come back again on time.

The Lord saves us from our sins on time.

The Lord cleanses us from our sins on time.

You and I are not always on time.

We don't always eat on time.

We don't always go to bed on time.

We don't always say the right words on time.

We don't always do the right things on time.

We don't always help someone on time.

We don't always go to church on time.

We don't always pray on time.

The Lord is always on time to answer our prayers.

He came to this world on time to save us from our sins.

He went back to heaven on time.

The Lord gives us His Holy Spirit on time.

The Lord heals us on time.

The Lord allowed us to be born into this world on time.

The Lord allows us to prosper on time.

The Lord shows us his mercy on time.

The Lord forgives us of our sins on time.

We are not always merciful on time.

We are not always forgiving on time.

We don't always tell the truth on time.

We are not always loving on time.

Our Lord and Savior Jesus Christ is always on time in every word that He says and in every thing that he does.

Jesus will supply all of our needs on time.

Jesus is never slack in what He says and does.

Money

Money will cause many people to feel good.

Money will cause many people to get through the day.

Money will get many people what they want.

Money will get many people what they need.

Money will cause many people to work hard.

The love of money will cause many people to kill.

The love of money will cause many people to steal.

The love of money will cause many women to prostitute themselves.

The love of money will cause many rich people to oppress the poor.

The love of money will cause many people to rob God.

We need money to help us to survive in this world.

We need money to buy the things we need.

If we use money in the right way, it will be a blessing from the Lord.

Money can cheer us up when we get some.

Many people will use their money in the wrong ways.

Many people will buy alcohol with their money.

Many people will buy cigarettes with their money.

Many people will buy drugs with their money.

Many people will buy sex with their money.

Many people will buy guns with their money.

Many people will try to buy friends with their money.

Many people will try to buy love with their money.

The love of money has destroyed many people's lives.

Many people will gamble with their money.

Many people have abandoned their families for the love of money.

Many people will tell lies for the love of money.

Even Jesus Christ was betrayed by Judas for the love of money.

No one can worship God and money at the same time.

Many people will use other people for their money.

Many people will get married for the love of money.

Many people will divorce their spouse for the love of money.

Many women will sell their babies for the love of money.

Many people will sell their souls to the devil for the love of money.

The Darkness of Sin

The darkness of sin will blind our spiritual eyes if we don't keep our eyes on Jesus.

The darkness of sin will control our minds if we don't keep our minds on Jesus.

The darkness of sin will control our hearts if we don't meditate on Jesus.

The darkness of sin doesn't care about how educated we are.

The darkness of sin doesn't care about how young we are.

The darkness of sin doesn't care about how old we are.

The darkness of sin doesn't care about how rich we are.

The darkness of sin doesn't care about how poor we are.

The darkness of sin doesn't care about how healthy we are.

The darkness of sin doesn't care about how sick we are.

The darkness of sin doesn't care about how good we are.

The darkness of sin doesn't care about how bad we are.

The darkness of sin tempted Jesus Christ, Our Lord, in the wilderness.

The darkness of sin depressed Jesus in the Garden of Gethsemane.

The darkness of sin crucified Jesus.

The darkness of sin doesn't care about putting out our lights.

Jesus Christ was a sinless man who gave us victory over the darkness of sin.

Jesus rose from the grave to give us victory over the darkness of sin.

If we close our eyes, we won't see anything.

If we can't see, we won't know where to go.

If we can't see anything, we are limited in what we can do.

There is nothing good about the darkness of sin.

It blinds us to the light of God's holy word.

The blind can't lead the blind out of darkness.

Many people are living in darkness right now in the heart of the church.

They go to church with no changed heart to repent.

Darkness can appear as a green light shining over brown grass to make it look like it's green grass.

Darkness is very deceptive every day.

God's holy word will let us know the difference between the light and the darkness of sin.

Off the Face of the Earth

Many people are driving so fast on the road, it's like they're trying to drive off the face of the earth.

They are only driving on their regular routine of going to many of the same places over and over again.

Many people are traveling here and there like they are trying to travel off the face of the earth.

So many planes are flying as if they want to fly us off the face of the earth.

Many astronauts have traveled off the face of the earth.

They all had to come back to the earth to keep on living.

If they stayed in outer space too long, they would die because they ran out of oxygen, food and water to drink.

The only way we can get off the face of the earth is through our Christian journey that will one day take us to heaven if we are saved in Jesus Christ.

Many people will climb the highest mountains as if they want to get off the face of the earth.

Many people will live in the tallest buildings as if they want to live off the face of the earth.

There is only one road that will one day take us off the face of the earth.

There is only one travel agent who can one day book us to travel off the face of the earth.

Many people will ride on your bumper as if they want to bump you off the face of the earth.

Jesus Christ, our Lord and Savior, will come back again one day and take all of His children off the face of the earth.

We can only hope and pray that we will be in that number to travel back to heaven with Jesus and all of His angels.

When Jesus comes back and takes us off the face of the earth, we won't run out of anything or need to come back to earth.

We are not like the astronauts who have to come back after they leave the earth.

Jesus will give us everything we need to leave the face of the earth.

Insecure

Many people will feel insecure about the way they look.

Many people will feel insecure about who they are.

Many people will feel insecure about their health.

Many people will feel insecure about their weight.

Many people will feel insecure about their height.

Many people will feel insecure about their jobs.

Many people will feel insecure about their businesses.

Many people will feel insecure about their marriages.

Many people will feel insecure about relationships with others.

Everybody may feel insecure about something.

Many people will feel insecure about their lives.

Many people will feel insecure about this world.

Many people will feel insecure about their faith in the Lord when trials come their way.

We live in an insecure world every day.

Bad things can happen so unexpectedly.

We just don't know what will happen next.

Many people will feel insecure about their financial needs.

Many people will feel insecure about their emotional needs.

Many people will feel insecure about their physical needs.

Many people will feel insecure about spiritual needs.

Natural disasters can make us feel insecure.

Sickness can make us feel insecure.

Political arguments can make us feel insecure.

If we are anchored in the Lord, we should not feel insecure regardless of what comes our way.

Jesus Christ, our Lord and Savior, is our one hundred percent security every day.

Fear

We all can fear something.

We all can fear a tornado.

We all can fear a forest fire.

We all can fear a hungry bear.

We all can fear a hungry lion.

We all can fear a poisonous snake.

We all can fear a mean dog.

We all can fear cancer.

We all can fear flu.

We all can fear the Corona Virus.

We all can fear a sickness.

We all can fear death.

We all need to fear God and keep His commandments.

This is a good kind of fear.

This kind of fear won't worry us and stress us.

We all can fear something.

Jesus Christ, our Lord and Savior, had to face up to the temptation of fear in the Garden of Gethsemane.

Peter, one of Jesus' disciples, denied Jesus three times because of his fear of being killed if he said he was one of Jesus' disciples.

We all can fear getting rejected.

We all can fear getting turned down.

We all can fear losing our eyesight.

We all can fear losing our hearing.

We all can fear losing a job.

We all can fear losing our house.

We all can fear going to jail.

We all can fear losing a loved one.

Many children will fear their parents.

Many parents will fear their children.

We all can fear the thunder and lightning.

We all can fear getting caught doing something wrong.

We all can fear getting our hearts broken.

We all need to fear God, which is a good kind of fear that is good for our souls.

Do We Crucify Jesus Today?

We know that the people of the world crucify Jesus by the way they live their selfish lives.

Do we crucify Jesus if we assume things about someone else without having any evidence?

Do we crucify Jesus if we say something to cause someone to look stupid?

Do we crucify Jesus if we are jealous of someone else?

Do we crucify Jesus if we talk bad about someone else, even if it's true?

Do we crucify Jesus if we hurt someone's feelings, especially on purpose?

Do we crucify Jesus if we look down on someone else?

Do we crucify Jesus if we doubt what He can do for us?

Do we crucify Jesus if we are opinionated?

Do we crucify Jesus if we show no respect for others?

Do we crucify Jesus if we joke about someone else?

Do we crucify Jesus by not helping someone in need?

Do we crucify Jesus if we believe that we are better than someone else?

When Jesus lived on earth, He was our living example of how to love everybody all the same.

Jesus loved everybody, even his enemies.

There is nothing good about crucifixion.

The Roman soldiers were very cruel to Jesus.

We must be careful not to be cruel to Jesus by the way we live our lives.

The people of the world crucify Jesus every day, but we know that we serve a risen Jesus Christ who overcame this world with victory over our sins.

Let us not be like the people of the world.

Carnal-minded People

Carnal-minded people don't care about getting to know the Lord Jesus Christ.

Carnal-minded people don't care about loving and obeying the Lord Jesus Christ.

Carnal-minded people don't care about spiritual things.

Carnal-minded people don't care about changing from their wicked ways.

Carnal-minded people don't care about denying themselves.

Carnal-minded people don't care about studying the bible.

Carnal-minded people don't care about loving their neighbors.

Carnal-minded people don't care about living right.

Carnal-minded people will choose to do evil.

Carnal-minded people are full of themselves.

Carnal-minded people don't care about doing good things in Jesus' name.

Carnal-minded people will do good things to make a name for themselves.

Carnal-minded people will lay up their treasures in this world.

Carnal-minded people will live to please this world.

Carnal-minded people will only serve this world.

Carnal-minded people don't care about breaking God's commandments.

Carnal-minded people will not confess and repent of their sins.

Carnal-minded people will not go to heaven.

Carnal-minded people don't care about being lost in their sins.

Carnal-minded people don't care about being saved in Jesus Christ.

Carnal-minded people will live in pleasure.

Carnal-minded people will live in their sins.

Carnal-minded people will despise spiritual-minded people.

Carnal-minded people will put their trust in this world.

Spiritual-minded people live their new lives unto the Lord.

Any One of Us

Any one of us could hold onto a bad habit if we don't give it to Jesus to help us to let go of the bad habit.

Any one of us could worry about things if we don't put our trust in Jesus to take our worries away.

Any one of us could make a mistake because we are not perfect and cannot do everything right all of the time.

Any one of us could make a bad choice if we don't stay prayed up and ask Jesus to help us make good choices.

Any one of us could say something wrong if we don't ask Jesus to help us say the right words.

Any one of us could think bad thoughts if we don't keep our minds on Jesus Christ.

Any one of us could fall into sin if we don't study God's holy word and ask Jesus to give us strength.

Any one of us could be tempted by the devil.

We have some weaknesses that we need to give to Jesus so He can help us to overcome them.

Any one of us can confess and repent of our sins unto Jesus Christ.

Any one of us can choose to believe in Jesus Christ and be saved.

Any one of us can work out our own soul's salvation by choosing to live a renewed life in Jesus Christ.

I Took a Lot of Chances

I took a lot of chances that could have caused me to lose my life, because I was young and ignorant in many ways.

I took a lot of chances and didn't give it a second thought.

I took a lot of chances and didn't care.

A lot of those chances I took were caused by the way I lived my life.

It's a miracle that I am still alive today.

I now know what a fool I was.

I know the right way to live now, and I don't want to ever again do those foolish things I used to do.

I thank the Lord for giving me a chance to live for Him and to know His holy word.

I know today that taking chances is not always a good thing to do.

The Lord didn't let my chances take my life.

My eyes are open today, and now I can see the chances I take.

The chances I take today are good because I live my life unto the Lord.

When I took a chance with Jesus Christ, my Lord, it was the best chance that I've ever taken.

I have no regrets at all.

Thanks to Jesus, I've learned to wise up and not take any more bad chances that I'm aware of.

I took a lot of chances when I was young and inexperienced with a lot of things in life.

Jesus has paid my price for the bad chances I took.

Children

When we were little children, we did a lot of bad things because we just didn't know any better.

We did those bad things out of pure ignorance day after day.

We believed that what we were doing was all right to do.

We believed that the bad words we said were all right to say.

We believed that we were good children in every way, until we got ourselves into some trouble.

A lot of us weren't as fortunate as other little children who didn't do a lot of foolish things because they were raised in the Lord.

We are so very fortunate today to be children of God.

We are children who are doing a lot of good things.

We are no longer so ignorant and not know right from wrong.

Today we are spiritually mature children who live in the spirit of God.

When we were little children, we didn't think about growing up and being responsible for what we say and do.

Today we are children of God.

We know what it means to be responsible for what we say and do.

We are no longer little children of the flesh.

Today we are children of the spirit of God, who gave us His only begotten Son to save us from our sins.

Your Marvelous Gospel

O Lord, you brought me into our marvelous gospel that changed my life so much for the better.

I was spiritually blind, and didn't know that You longed to bring me into Your marvelous gospel.

Your marvelous gospel, my Lord Jesus Christ, opened my eyes to see that You love me with an everlasting love that's way beyond my mother's love.

O, my Lord and Savior Jesus Christ, You are the good news in my eyes and ears, and I can see and hear your gospel in Your holy word.

O Lord, You brought me into Your marvelous gospel that I don't deserve to know because I loved living in darkness like it was heaven on earth.

You, my Lord, are my real, true heaven on earth, where Your marvelous gospel is for all the world to know.

O Lord, You are the marvelous gospel that's eternal beyond all of my days.

If Jesus is Not in It

A poem could be great to the world but worthless to Jesus if He is not in it.

A book could be great to the world but worthless to Jesus if He is not in it.

A song could be great to the world but worthless to Jesus if He is not in it.

A speech could be great to the world but worthless to Jesus if He is not in it.

A talent could be great to the world but worthless to Jesus if He is not in it.

A skill could be great to the world but worthless to Jesus if He is not in it.

Knowledge could be great to the world but worthless to Jesus if He is not in it.

Your Holy Word

Your holy word, O Lord, was life in the past that many people lived by.

Your holy word, O Lord, is life in the present that many people live by.

O Lord, Your holy word will be life in the future that many people will live by.

When I read Your holy word, O Lord, I can feel life.

When I read Your holy word, O Lord, I can see life.

Your holy word is full of life and full of truth.

Your holy word, O Lord, was truth in the past.

Your holy word, O Lord, is truth in the present.

Your holy word, O Lord, will be truth in the future.

Your holy word, O Lord, comes from You who was made flesh to be the living word of God.

Your holy word, O Lord, is You — the way, the truth, and the life.

Your holy word, O Lord, is everlasting.

Heaven and earth would pass away before Your word would change.

Your word, O Lord, is forever the same.

Dreams and Reality

Dreams can be like a soft pillow to lay your head on.

Reality can be like a hard rock to lay your head on.

Dreams can be like a warm gentle breeze blowing on you and me.

Reality can be like the hot sun shining down on you and me.

Dreams can come and go.

Reality can surely stay around for a long time.

We can see dreams in our sleep.

We can see reality in our everyday life.

Dreams can be no big deal.

Reality can be hard to deal with.

Dreams can cause us to think about what can happen.

Reality can cause us to know what will happen.

Dreams can make us feel good.

Reality can throw cold water on us.

Dreams can have an effect on our sleep.

Reality can have an effect on our lives.

Dreams can give us something to think about.

Reality can give us something to never forget.

Jesus Christ is coming back again to be like a dream coming true.

Going through trials for Jesus' name sake is reality to everyone who loves and obeys Jesus.

Dreams can be like a good sneeze.

Reality can be like looking in the mirror and seeing yourself and no one else.

Who Can Answer Jesus' Questions?

Who can answer Jesus' questions?

Jesus asked the Pharisees some questions that they could not answer because they did not understand.

If Jesus asked you and me a question, could we answer Him?

Oh, we have less than a slim chance of being able to answer Jesus' questions that no man can answer.

Jesus' questions will leave us speechless like the Pharisees who were left speechless all day and all night long.

Many people will question Jesus without a second thought.

They will linger on it and try to sort out their problems themselves.

Who can answer Jesus' questions, when He already knows the answers?

We can go here and there looking for the answers to His questions that we can't bear to answer.

Jesus can always answer our questions; they are not too complicated for Him to answer no matter where we live.

You and I are not worthy to answer Jesus' questions that will only puzzle us.

Jesus can always answer all of our questions so dear.

Life Doesn't

Life doesn't have impurities — we have impurities.

Life doesn't make choices — we make choices.

Life doesn't get weary — we get weary.

Life doesn't have problems — we have problems.

Life doesn't fall asleep — we fall asleep.

Life doesn't have troubles — we have troubles.

Life doesn't have trials — we have trials.

Life doesn't pretend — we can pretend.

Life doesn't grieve — we grieve.

Life doesn't die — we can die.

Life doesn't make mistakes — we make mistakes.

Life doesn't sin against the Lord — we sin against the Lord.

Jesus Christ is the source of life.

Yesterday, Today, and Tomorrow

Yesterday has passed by us and gone to a place of no return.

Yesterday has paid us its debt of the past.

Yesterday was the Lord's day to help us to overcome obstacles.

Today is present with us to know that we are still alive.

Today will bark at us like a dog to let us know that we need to be aware of what today might bring us.

Today is the Lord's day for us to know that He is still in charge of everything today.

Tomorrow is a day that we must wait on to see what it will be like.

Tomorrow is watching out for us to make good choices to help us to live to see tomorrow.

Tomorrow is the Lord's day and He will still be Lord of lords and King of kings.

Who Am I to Question You, My Lord

Who am I to Question You, my Lord Jesus Christ who is always faithful?

Who am I to Question You, my Lord Jesus who is all-wise.

Who am I to Question You, my Lord Jesus who is all-knowing.

Who am I to Question You, my Lord Jesus who is all-holy.

Who am I to Question You, my Lord Jesus who is all perfection.

Who am I to Question You, my Lord Jesus who is all righteous.

Who am I to Question You, my Lord Jesus who is all-powerful.

Who am I to Question You, my Lord Jesus who is all mighty.

Who am I to Question You, my Lord Jesus who is all truthful.

Who am I to Question You, my Lord Jesus who is all trustworthy.

Who am I to Question You, my Lord Jesus who is all forgiving.

Who am I to Question You, my Lord Jesus who is all life.

Who am I to Question You, my Lord Jesus who is all merciful.

Who am I to Question You, my Lord Jesus who is all victorious.

Who am I to Question You, my Lord Jesus who is all real.

Who am I to Question You, my Lord Jesus who is all freedom.

Who am I to Question You, my Lord Jesus who is all graciousness.

Who am I to Question You, my Lord Jesus who is all good.

Who am I to Question You, my Lord Jesus who is all glorious.

Who am I to Question You, my Lord Jesus who is all fair.

Who am I to Question You, my Lord Jesus who is all loving.

The Sky Hovers Over

The sky hovers over this uncertain world where the economy is pulling people down like crabs in a barrel.

The sky hovers over every sound of life that voices its presence from day to day.

Under the sky is where sin preys on you and me, trying to get us to trespass against God's holy law.

The sky hovers over the great and small.

We must love Jesus Christ and keep His holy law in our hearts so that Jesus will give us the victory, if we confess and repent of our sins.

The sky hovers over the living and the dead that Jesus is always ahead of to know all who are saved in Him.

The sky hovers over every word that we say and every thing that we do from day to day.

Jesus hovers over our salvation in Him who is God's Son and God's grace.

A Dark World

We are living in a dark world of sin that will get darker and darker before the end of this dark world.

This dark world is darker than the darkest night, that is like the sand running out of our hourglass.

We are living in these very dark last days that will get darker and darker just like the bible says.

Jesus will not let this dark world put out His light that stays bright in every heart that believes in Him and keeps His commandments.

We are all like sheep that are lost without Jesus Christ leading us and guiding us to put all of trust in Him in this dark world.

This world will get darker and darker in every way, but Jesus will stretch out His hand to save you and me from being lost in sin.

Jesus can do anything but fail you and me.

Jesus is Bigger Than the Storm

Jesus is bigger than the storm.

A storm doesn't have a chance against Jesus Christ, our Lord and savior.

No matter what the storm is, Jesus is in the midst of it and will bring us through.

The storm knows that Jesus is bigger and will calm it down.

Storms will come and storms will go, but Jesus is forever present in and out of the storms.

Jesus is bigger than any storm from the north, south, east or west side of this world.

No storm has ever defeated Jesus Christ, our Lord, who has faced the most terrible storm.

Jesus went through that storm for me and you, because we could not make it through.

Jesus is bigger than the storm, and the storm will obey Him.

Give Jesus the glory and the praise.

Everlasting

One day soon, we will be everlasting in Jesus Christ who lends us all that we have in this world.

One day soon, we will be everlasting beyond the gates of pearl where all the holy saints will live forever and ever with Jesus Christ for being saved in Him.

From everlasting to everlasting, God will make us like the angels in heaven above this sinful world where we are living off of God's love.

Long and everlasting is the Lord Jesus Christ, who will never leave us or forsake us in this life.

One day soon, we will be everlasting beyond the stars and no lost soul can know the feelings in our hearts when we will be caught up on the clouds of glory.

You Were with Me

O Lord, you were with me in all of my past years when I didn't know how dear You were to me.

O Lord, you were with me in all of my past years when I didn't know that I would make it this far in this wicked world.

You, O Lord, didn't leave me all alone to be knocked down and kicked around by the devil who is known to steal, rob and kill anyone he can.

O Lord, you were with me in a sinful land where I just didn't see my way out of the troubles that I put myself in.

You, O Lord, made a way out of my troubles for me when I was walking on thin ice that could have broken and let me drown in my sins.

O Lord, you were with me and led me to walk on your holy ground where I could love and obey You through my ups and downs, even in the household of faith.

O Lord, You open doors for me to live and see this day that You made for me.

I know that You were always with me, even when I just didn't know You like I do today.

I am a Christian Black Man

I am a Christian Black man with a dream to lead me through an opinionated world of me existing because of God's love for me.

I am a Christian Black man to face up to myself to love or hate who I am.

This world will stress out my existence from day to day.

I can only be me and love or hate myself in the presence of opinionated people who don't know me.

I am a Christian Black man who is not here by accident.

God came up with a good idea to create me like He wanted to.

God didn't make a mistake when the devil made a mistake to judge me and hate me who can choose to love God and my neighbors.

The devil is my true enemy.

He knows that God didn't create me to be an empty shell.

The sand can run out of an hourglass.

A star can fall from the sky.

A shadow can disappear.

I am a Christian Black man who God created for eternity beyond the things that are temporary and can end.

I am a Christian Black man who can love everybody, even though some people hate me.

I am somebody to God, even if nobody else cares.

I am a human being who God created in His image, and I think, reason and live to worship Him.

I am not an animal that can't think and can't reason things out.

When you see me, you can see that I am a human being like you.

You may want to hate me or kill me for no good reason, even though you may believe you have a good reason.

I am a Christian Black man all day and all night long.

My color won't change for you, even if you have a problem with the color of my skin.

Jesus Christ, my Lord and Savior, died on the cross for my sins too.

He didn't leave me out of His salvation because I am black.

When you see me in heaven, don't be shocked.

Heaven is for the Christian black man too.

I love who I am, and I am black, not Asian, Jewish, white or Arab, or any other race.

If you have a problem with me being black, then you need to talk to God about it.

I am a Christian Black man who was born to be black.

Life welcomes me into this world because I was meant to be here to do God's will.

Being black is a problem for anyone who doesn't love God.

God says that if you say you love Him who you don't see but hate your brother who you do see, then you are a liar.

I am your black brother who you do see.

I am a Christian Black man existing to live in a sinful world where the devil is my real, true enemy who tries to cause my soul to be lost.

I am a Christian Black man walking through the wilderness of the uncertain that loves to try to make me think living my life is in vain.

God has made my life worth living to be like the sound of gospel songs.

My blackness will follow me wherever I go.

It will attract some attention, and some will accept me for being black.

I am a Christian Black man who is a controversial subject to the devil.

He knows that if I love Jesus Christ, he lost his victory over me.

I am a Christian Black man who is no island sitting all alone in the middle of the sea.

God will stand me up in the middle of his angels every day.

God created me to be a black man who he approves of in this world and in the new world to come one day.

Could it be profound to God to create a black man to be different from all other men of different races?

God is matchless, so who can question God for creating a black man like me?

I am a Christian Black man who is tossed on every side of the world by people stereotyping me like poisonous fumes coming out of an exhaust pipe.

My Lord and Savior Jesus Christ has renewed my life for me.

His love is just like clean air to breathe in and out day after day.

Ignorance will conspire against me and injustice will gladly accuse me of being a Christian black man day after day in a world that shows favoritism to the privileged.

I am a Christian Black man who God favors to live in this world and claim my existence.

I am a Christian Black man who the sun will shine down on with respect.

The full white moon will glow down on me with respect.

The rainbow will arch up high over me with respect.

The rain and snow will fall down on me with respect.

Nature will surround me with respect.

Nature will treat me as no less of a man than any other man of any race, creed or culture of men.

I am a Christian Black man for others to see and greatly accept when Jesus comes back again.

Keeping God's Commandments

Keeping God's commandments will set us free from idol worship.

Keeping God's commandments will set us free from pride.

Keeping God's commandments will set us free from jealousy.

Keeping God's commandments will set us free from strife.

Keeping God's commandments will set us free from rebellion.

Keeping God's commandments will set us free from wars.

Keeping God's commandments will set us free from bloodshed.

Keeping God's commandments will set us free from prejudice.

Keeping God's commandments will set us free from deception.

Keeping God's commandments will set us free from hatred.

Keeping God's commandments will set us free from heartache.

Keeping God's commandments will set us free from crimes.

Keeping God's commandments will set us free from lies.

Keeping God's commandments will set us free from fornication.

Keeping God's commandments will set us free from adultery.

Keeping God's commandments will set us free from greed.

Keeping God's commandments will set us free from abuse.

Keeping God's commandments will set us free from selfishness.

Jesus Christ, our Lord, says that if you love Him, you will keep His commandments.

Keeping God's commandments will keep us free from holding grudges.

Keeping God's commandments will set us free from envy.

Keeping God's commandments will set us free from lawlessness.

Keeping God's commandments will set us free from global warming.

Keeping God's commandments will set us free from trouble.

Keeping God's commandments will set us free from injustice.

Keeping God's commandments will set us free from discrimination.

Keeping God's commandments will set us free from slavery.

Keeping God's commandments will set us free from living in sin.

Keeping God's commandments is freedom every day.

None of us can be free without keeping God's commandments.

Being a slave to sin is breaking God's commandments.

Keeping God's commandments will set us free from fear.

Keeping God's commandments will set us free from conflicts.

Keeping God's commandments is freedom all around the world.

It's No Mistake

It's no mistake that we are in one another's lives.

The Lord doesn't make mistakes.

It's the Lord who brought us into one another's lives for a very good reason.

We are not in one another's lives by luck.

The Lod knew that we would be able to put up with one another.

The Lord know that we would learn something from one another.

It's the Lord who brought us across one another's path.

The Lord knew that we would love each other in some kind of way.

The Lord knew that we would come together for the Sabbath school lessons.

The Lord knew that we would come together for the eleven o'clock Sabbath sermons.

The Lod knew that we would come together for communion.

The Lord also brought other people into our lives to be a blessing to us.

The Lord knew that we would be a blessing to one another.

The Lord makes no mistakes when He brings people into our lives, even some people we may not like.

The Lord's reasons are always good and right, especially for us Christians to be a witness of Him before others in our lives.

The Lord makes no mistakes when he brings you and me into each other's lives.

The Lord knew that we would learn from our mistakes and make it right with one another sooner or later.

The Lord knew that we would learn to love one another, especially in the household of faith.

The Lord put us all at the right place at the right time.

The Lord knew that we all would be good for one another in some kind of way.

The Lord has given us all the opportunity to love one another and to be His disciples.

The Lord doesn't make mistakes.

We can make a mistake when we don't trust the Lord to bring people into our lives, whether they are good or bad.

We don't want to believe that the Lord will bring someone bad into our lives.

The Lord knows if we can bear that bad person in our lives.

The Lord knows if that bad person will change from living in sin when seeing our example.

None of us is perfect and we can see that in one another in some kind of way.

The Lord knows that our sins are not greater than our love for one another.

The Lord says that love covers a multitude of sins.

The Lord knows that we can bear one another's burdens.

The Lord makes no mistakes.

Even before the Lord brought us together, He knew that we were not going to do everything right, but He knew what He was doing when he brought us all together in His holy name.

Rich with Spiritual Things

We may be poor and not have a lot of money, but we are rich with love for loving Jesus Christ.

We may be poor and not have a lot of material things, but we are rich with spiritual things for being saved in Jesus Christ.

We Christians are rich with joy in Jesus, even though we live in a world of sorrows.

We Christians are rich with peace, even though we live in a world of troubled times.

We Christians are rich with temperance, even though we live in a world of so many uncontrolled people.

We Christians are rich with truth, even though we live in a world of so many people telling lies.

We Christians are rich with patience, even though we live in a world of so many people wanting things so fast.

We Christians are rich with wisdom, even though we live in a world filled with so many foolish people who aren't aware of their surroundings.

We Christians are rich with bible knowledge, even though we live in a world of so many people who don't know what is right and what is wrong.

We Christians are rich with humility, even though we live in a world of so many proud people.

We Christians are rich with giving, even though we live in a world of so many selfish people.

We Christians are rich with keeping God's holy law, even though we live in a world of so many people breaking God's law.

We Christians are rich with compassion, even though we living in a world of so many people who show no pity.

We Christians are rich with contentment, even though we living in a world of so many greedy people only out for worldly gain.

We Christians are rich with equality, even though we live in a world of so many people who show others no respect.

We Christians are rich with forgiveness, even though we live in a world where so many people hold grudges.

We Christians are rich with spiritual things, even though we live in a world of so many people who hate spirituals things.

We Christians are rich with the fruit of the spirit, even though we are living in a world of so many people who reject the Holy Spirit.

We Christians are rich with faith in Jesus, even though we live in a world of so many people who don't believe in Jesus Christ.

We Christians are spiritually rich.

We don't have to worry about ever running out of spiritual things.

Many financially rich people will worry about running out of their riches.

We spiritually rich people can deposit our riches up in the bank of heaven where no thief can ever rob.

We Christians are rich with encouragement, even though we are living in a world of so many people who love to tear people down.

There are many Christians who are spiritually rich but not financially rich.

Deep Within Ourselves

If we truly look deep within ourselves, we will like or we won't like who we see.

If we are truly a child of God, we will love that we are truly like Jesus Christ.

If we truly look deep within ourselves, we will see our sins that we need to confess and repent of unto the Lord.

Knowing a lot of bible scriptures doesn't define you and me or make us always be like Jesus.

Praying good prayers doesn't define you and me or make us always be like Jesus.

Teaching a good Sabbath school lesson doesn't define anyone or make us always be like Jesus.

Going vegetarian doesn't define anyone or make them always be like Jesus.

Preaching a good sermon doesn't define anyone or make them always be like Jesus.

We don't very often like to look deep within ourselves because we really don't want to see something there that is not like Jesus.

We may try to look deep within someone else to find something bad within them to try to make ourselves look good.

The Lord means what He says when He tells you and me that we must deny ourselves and pick up our cross to follow Him.

We can want to follow Jesus in the bible scriptures.

We can want to follow Jesus in the sermons we hear.

We don't always truly see that we need to follow Jesus in the words we say and in the things we do.

If we truly look deep within ourselves, we will see that we still have a long way to go to always be like Jesus.

Before we were born into this sinful world, Jesus knew that we would not always be aware of every word we say and every thing we do.

If we could see our real, true selves all the time, we would be crying out to Jesus all the time and asking Him to forgive us of our sins.

It's so easy to try to look deep within someone else to try to find some fault.

To look deep within ourselves is to accept that we are sinners who need to confess and repent of our sins.

To look deep within ourselves is to block out everyone else from our minds and see only ourselves so we can admit that we are sinners needing Jesus Christ to cleanse us of our sins.

If we truly look deep within ourselves, we can give Jesus a chance to come into our hearts where He is needed most.

We cannot hide behind our outward good words and good deeds.

Only Jesus truly knows what we are made of every day.

There are some things deep within our hearts that we are not aware of.

Deep within our hearts is a lifetime cleansing of our sins that only Jesus can do.

Actions

Actions can be questioned.

Many people will do something good for the wrong reasons.

Laughter is supposed to be a good action, but many people laugh about doing something wrong.

We must defend ourselves and protect ourselves and that is a good thing, but many people think this is a bad action.

A man can be eating in a restaurant with a woman who is not his wife or girlfriend and someone else may see him and believe that something is going on between them.

His actions will look bad to that person who doesn't have any proof about what is truly going on.

His actions are good if they are just friends, even though his actions might look bad to someone else who doesn't know him.

A woman may come to church in a short dress, and some might believe that she is trying to pick up a man in the church.

Her actions are good if that is the only clean dress she can wear because she didn't have time to do her laundry.

Someone else might see this as a bad action on her part because she wore that short dress.

A man may come to church wearing a casual shirt and casual pants.

Someone might see this as a bad action because he didn't come to church wearing a suit.

His actions might be good if his heart is in the right place in coming to church.

We can't judge one another's actions; only the Lord always knows whether our actions are good or bad.

A child might be misbehaving, and someone might believe that the child is mean.

The misbehaving child's actions can look bad, even though the child may have been through some trauma.

A woman may get an abortion, and someone else may see it to be a bad action.

The woman might have been raped and she couldn't bear to birth a baby that came from that action.

It may be a good action on her part if she knows she cannot love and care for the child.

A couple can look so happy together when they're walking down the street holding hands.

This can look like a good action, but their children might see it as a bad action because they know that their parents are only pretending to love each other out in public.

When they are at home, behind closed doors, their children see them arguing with each other.

Actions can sometimes be deceiving.

Some things that many people do are only a pretense.

Their actions are not real, even though it may look real to people who see them.

Jesus Christ, our Lord, was always real in His actions that had no flaws of sin.

Common Sense

Common sense will tell us to help somebody if we can help him or her.

Common sense will tell us to slow down.

Common sense will tell us not to tailgate anyone on the road.

Common sense will tell us to drive the speed limit.

Common sense will tell us to not talk too much.

Common sense will tell us to listen.

Common sense will tell us to be nice to people.

Common sense will tell us to treat people right.

Common sense will tell us to get our rest.

Common sense will tell us to tell the truth.

Common sense will tell us to not over do things.

Common sense will tell us to pay our bills.

Common sense will tell us to return what belongs to the Lord.

Common sense will tell us to not form opinions about others.

Common sense will tell us to take a shower.

Common sense will tell us to brush our teeth.

Common sense will tell us to comb our hair.

Common sense will tell us to take care of ourselves.

Common sense will tell us to put on our cloths.

Common sense will tell us to be faithful to our spouse.

Common sense will tell us to not make our children angry.

Common sense will tell us to keep our distance from angry people.

Common sense will tell us to treat our pets right.

Common sense will tell us to not use anyone.

Common sense will tell us to not want what belongs to others.

Common sense will tell us to not trust foolish people.

Common sense will tell us to love and obey Jesus Christ.

Common sense will tell us to love our neighbors.

Common sense will tell us to not eat too much food.

Common sense will tell us to eat the right food.

Common sense will tell us to cover our mouths when we cough.

Common sense will tell us to wash our hands.

Common sense will tell us to drink plenty of water.

Common sense will tell us to not get overweight.

Common sense will tell us to exercise.

Common sense will tell us to get some sunshine.

Common sense will tell us to not work too hard.

Common sense will tell us to not be overly righteous.

Common sense will tell us to be at church on time.

Common sense will tell us to read the bible for ourselves.

Common sense will tell us to not to worry.

Common sense will tell us to get some help if we need it.

Common sense will tell us to see a doctor if we are sick.

Common sense will tell us to not brag about ourselves.

Common sense will tell us to not brag about anyone else.

Common sense is from the Lord, who gives us common sense to survive in this world.

Common sense will tell us to not touch the hot fire.

Common sense will tell us to lock our doors.

Common sense will tell us to wash our clothes.

Common sense will tell us to be careful about what we say.

Common sense will tell us to be careful about what we do.

Common sense will tell us to trust the Lord.

Common sense will tell us to pray to the Lord.

Common sense will tell us to live our lives unto the Lord.

Not everyone uses their common sense.

Many people will act like they don't have any common sense at all.

Common sense makes things clear to us.

Common sense will tell us to be real with people.

Jesus Didn't Let the Devil Kill Me

The devil tried to kill me with a virus that gave me a high fever.

Jesus didn't let the devil kill me.

The devil tried to kill me when I was locked up in the trunk of an old car.

Jesus didn't let the devil kill me.

The devil tried to kill me when a group of men beat me up.

Jesus didn't let the devil kill me.

The devil tried to kill me when someone had a gun to my head.

Jesus didn't let the devil kill me.

The devil tried to kill me when I fell asleep behind the wheel of my car.

Jesus didn't let the devil kill me.

The devil tried to kill me when someone had a knife to my throat.

Jesus didn't let the devil kill me.

The devil hates to see me being alive this day.

He didn't want to see me living my life unto the Lord and Savior Jesus Christ.

The devil knew that when Jesus got ahold of me there would be no turning back for me.

Jesus didn't let the devil kill me because Jesus knew that I was living so ignorant in my sins.

Jesus is a second chance Lord and Savior to give me a chance to accept Him as my Lord and Savior or reject Him.

I'm so glad that I accepted Jesus Christ as my Lord and Savior when he gave me a second chance to confess and repent of my sins.

What Jesus did for me, He does the same for every ignorant person who just doesn't know better.

Everyone needs to get to know Jesus, who leaves no one out of His saving grace.

The Sleeping Saints

Jesus Christ will come back one day to wake up the sleeping saints.

Jesus will wake them up like they never slept even for one hour.

Right now, the sleeping saints know nothing and can do nothing.

They are sleeping away in Jesus' holy and precious name.

Many of the sleeping saints have been sleeping for thousands of years.

Many of the sleeping saints have been sleeping for hundreds of years.

Many of the sleeping saints have been sleeping for decades.

Many of the sleeping saints have been sleeping for months.

The sleeping saints are sealed for eternal life that they will one day wake up to see and live again.

The sleeping saints are so blessed to be sleeping as though time is standing still.

You and I may one day join the sleeping saints if Jesus doesn't come back while we are alive.

There will be some saints who will be alive to see Jesus Christ on the clouds of glory.

The sleeping saints will wake up out of their sleep when Jesus calls them to life so He can take them up on the clouds of glory up in the sky.

The sleeping saints will wake up in the first resurrection and will be so happy to see Jesus, along with the righteous living.

Pity and sorrow unto those who will wake up in the second resurrection to die again in the eternal death.

My Lord and Savior Jesus Christ

My Lord and Savior Jesus Christ, You are God's Son.

My Lord and Savior Jesus Christ, You are God's word.

My Lord and Savior Jesus Christ, You are God's love.

My Lord and Savior Jesus Christ, You are God's truth.

My Lord and Savior Jesus Christ, You are God's mercy.

My Lord and Savior Jesus Christ, You are God's peace.

My Lord and Savior Jesus Christ, You are God's glory.

My Lord and Savior Jesus Christ, You are God's grace.

My Lord and Savior Jesus Christ, You are God's goodness.

My Lord and Savior Jesus Christ, You are God's joy.

My Lord and Savior Jesus Christ, You are God's patience.

My Lord and Savior Jesus Christ, You are God's witness.

My Lord and Savior Jesus Christ, You are God's law.

My Lord and Savior Jesus Christ, You are God's justice.

My Lord and Savior Jesus Christ, You are God's judgment.

My Lord and Savior Jesus Christ, You are God's fairness.

My Lord and Savior Jesus Christ, You are God's faithful.

You are So Good to Me

O Lord, You may not answer my prayers when I want You to, but You are so good to answer my prayers on time when I need You most.

O Lord, You are so good to me all the time, even when time may seem to stand still and my prayers seem to not go anywhere.

O Lord, You are so good to me when I don't see my way so clear and don't know what to do.

You, O Lord, show me what I need to do to make my life better, day after day.

O Lord, Your blessings are extraordinary beyond my life that is ordinary.

I know that you are so good to me and bless me beyond my will that I cannot put my trust in.

I can always put my trust in You, my Lord Jesus Christ, who are so good to me even when I don't wait on You to answer my prayers.

It Means Nothing Much at All If Jesus is Not in It

Many people will say a lot of good words, but they mean nothing much at all if Jesus is not in the good words.

Many people will do a lot of good things, but they mean nothing much at all if Jesus is not in the good things that are done.

It's always good to speak Jesus' name, and it's always good to put Jesus into what we do.

It's Jesus who gives you and me the life, health and strength to say and do good things every day.

If Jesus is not in our words, then our words are worthless.

If Jesus is not in what we do, then our deeds are so worthless.

Many people don't believe in Jesus Christ, instead they believe in themselves like they're a god.

They believe in themselves to be diehard.

Many people will accomplish great things in life, but if Jesus is not in it there is no eternal value in those great things.

Our Faith is Being Tested

Our faith in Jesus is being tested in this coronavirus pandemic. We just don't know how long it will last.

Many people who don't have faith in Jesus will get depressed and just not know what to do.

We people of faith in Jesus know what to do day after day.

We know to keep our trust in Jesus to bring us through this new normal.

We must stay spiritually awake to know that this world will not get any better.

We Christians should really know about what is truly going on in this word.

We know that the devil's time is very short.

We should know that the devil is all about killing people with whatever he can use to kill as many people as possible.

We know that this coronavirus is of the devil.

The Lord permitted this virus to break out for a reason.

We don't always know about God's reasons for allowing bad things to happen.

Our faith in Jesus is being tested like Peter was tested when Jesus was taken captive by the soldiers.

Peter failed to say that he had been with Jesus.

We Christians know that it's our trying times, and we have to hold on to Jesus like never before.

We must show the world that we have peace of mind, regardless of all the people who are worried about whether they will die from this coronavirus.

Our faith in Jesus is being tested unto death.

Any one of us could get the coronavirus and die.

We must love and obey Jesus Christ, our Lord, even unto death.

Our faith in Jesus is being tested for the worst to come upon this world.

We must pray without ceasing.

We must be obedient unto the Lord in this world that will get no better.

We Christians know that the Holy Spirit is withdrawing from this world.

We know that probation is about to one day close on this world.

Our faith is being tested.

We are in the lion's den of this world.

We are in the furnace fire of this world.

Jesus is with us to the end.

Jesus shut the lion's mouth.

Jesus held back the fire in the furnace.

Jesus will do the same for us today.

www.ingramcontent.com/pod-product-compliance
Lightning Source LLC
Chambersburg PA
CBHW050041080526
44586CB00014B/1404